Searching for the Waters of Antiquity

A Story for Children of All Ages

Written and Illustrated
by
Shirley Ryan

Soul Moments Publishing
Petaluma, CA

Published by Soul Moments Publishing • P.O. Box 4763, Petaluma, CA 94955-4763 • telephone 707.775.4409
Printed in Hong Kong through Global Interprint, Inc. Santa Rosa, CA

Special discounts on bulk quantities of Soul Moments books are available to corporations, professional associations, and other organizations.
For details, contact the Director of Book Sales at Soul Moments Publishing, fax: 707.773.4624.

Ryan, Shirley
In Search of the Waters of Antiquity: A Follow-Along Meditation Process.--1st ed.

ISBN 0-9754196-0-9
1. Self-actualization (Psychology)   2. Spirituality   3. New Age

FIRST EDITION
First printing 2004

This book is dedicated with love to my daughter Dina and granddaughters Nicole, Sarah, and Victoria, through which I have the privilege to observe the unfolding of life.

They are the golden links that move across generational lines towards an ever higher evolving self.

Table of Contents

Author's Notes

Many years ago I sat in the backyard of my adopted Oklahoma home watching the dogs dash in and out of the bushes. I looked around the peaceful and beautifully landscaped yard. Ponds, waterfalls, flowers, and lush foliage dotted the walking paths of the serene setting I created to escape the mounting stress at work. My yard was my sanctuary, my peace and my joy. It seemed that the more stress I was under, the more I poured myself into that yard. I escaped into the beauty that surrounded me and it worked, for a while.

Reflecting back to the winter months before, it was clear that the beauty of my yard was not enough. Fatigue was a continuing problem for me and I was told to stay home from work and rest. I had trouble negotiating the stairs. Walking for any distance was a strain. I remembered some months before my physician had explained that if I didn't change my life style and reduce my stress, I would pay the consequences. Little did either of us know that I was already very ill, a tumor rested in the upper quadrant of my left lung. This can't wait; he said evenly, it is time to put your work life on hold. A trickle of fear ran down my spine as the full impact of what he was saying registered in my heart. I knew this was serious and I obediently did all that I was told to do in preparation for the surgery.

This included all sorts of alternative methods that I read about in health care books. One of those methods was meditation, breath work and the relaxation response. While I had practiced meditation periodically over the years, I never really saw myself as a person who meditates. I never made it a part of my self-image or self-care practices. But as the time for the surgery drew closer, I began to read everything I could that reflected the kind of alternative hope that I was sure would work for me. I meditated diligently to maintain a positive attitude throughout the grim news that seemed to bombard me daily.

My surgeon watched over me as I discussed my need to bring a meditation tape into the operating room to ensure that I would work well with him during surgery. I explained that I had carefully scripted a surgical accompaniment that would keep my body functioning within normal range in keeping with his plans for a successful procedure. Looking down, he curbed a smile as he agreed that he had heard of this kind of thing, but never personally experienced the process. He was guessing it was a West Coast thing…but he would do anything that would make me feel more comfortable. Time passed.

The physical trauma of the surgery was very invasive, but I was fortunate indeed. The surgery left me with a large scar, a small piece of my lung removed and with no other ill effects. The tumor was benign. Recuperation was ongoing and I was healing fast. I got well and was back to work in record time. Even so, I reflected on what my first doctor told me and I felt that he was right. I cashed in a CD (Certificate of Deposit), tied up loose ends and resigned my management position. I spent the next year meditating and drawing Mandalas to focus meditation more effectively. I exercised on a treadmill, ate good food, focused on living differently, staying in tune with my body and everything around me.

Then one day something meaningful happened that I would only later understand. In the heat of a summer day I went to the garage and found a turtle huddled in a corner. He looked pretty fried, so I put him in the backyard to cool off. Next year he was still there and so was a friend. A little story unfolded from that encounter which became the first part of this book. I wrote it down for my young granddaughters and eventually added sketches, then paintings to share the little story. I went back to work, but I still meditated, painted and drew Mandalas in my free time.

Over the next few years I trained to be a therapist, eventually returning to the West Coast, settling around family. Turning counseling skills into coaching, I cautiously went to work for a large organization. Mindful of past work experiences, I mapped out a plan to stay attuned to my body, my spirit and the practice of meditating. Several years ago I began a series of meditations that was somewhat different and I started getting ideas for paintings that were unusual. I would paint them and put them away, musing that they were a bit childlike or primitive in style. More and more images came to mind and I painted them, putting them in a shoebox for posterity. I didn't think of them much at all. They were too small to do anything with I thought. Then I was surprised when on two separate occasions, months apart, I sat up in the middle of the night and completely wrote part two and three of this book. Surprisingly the pictures, even the rather abstract ones fit perfectly with the stories.

What amazed me even more was the way I wrote the stories, especially the last one. I wrote furiously, the words didn't seem to register in my thoughts. My fingers flew across the page in a cursive rush of power and I had trouble keeping up with the flow of the pen against the paper. I was writing so automatically that I didn't even know what I was writing until I finished the last word and read the pages aloud to myself. Over the years, I would read them again, marveling that it could have come from my pen. My work and technical writing is in no way similar to the style in the story.

I played with the stories and the paintings, and eventually I put them into a computer program to enjoy. One day someone said they would like to read the little books, perhaps they would read it to their children. As time went on it was suggested that I combine the books. Many confessed that the story was a charming tale, and seemed to recover the childlike feeling in adults. So I proclaim this to be a story for children of all ages, a story for the kid inside us all.

Forward

I love stories. Stories are beautifully woven tapestries of characters, places, experiences, sights, sounds, colors and feelings that can reflect back to us a glimpse - or perhaps a full length mirror image! – of who we are at our core and guide us on our path of unfoldment.

This is a story for children ages eight to eighty. Yes, that's correct! Children who have lived eighty years on this green earth! The child is an energy, a being, an archetype that lives within us no matter how old we are. Can you remember a time when you were innocent, open and flexible? Can you remember a time when you were curious, full of questions, and wonder-full? Can you remember a time when you were playful, adventurous and trusting? These are all qualities of a child. If you are the kind of adult who is dismissive of child-like behavior and expression as silly and unproductive, I would encourage a reconsideration of this stance. The qualities of a child are important for learning, growing and discovering spiritual truths. Unfortunately, many of us have become disconnected from our own child-like nature through the process of enculturation, increasing responsibilities and the complexities of life. And the more disconnected we become we may experience a lack of joy, passion and meaning in life. This does not have to be so – we do not have to be immobilized by fear, tragedy or life circumstance!

"Searching for the Waters of Antiquity" offers all of us an invitation and a gift. To join Tag, the main character, in his search, we all have the opportunity to discover the waters that soothe, purify, nourish and re-vitalize. Allow yourself to flow with these waters, the Waters of Life, and be transported to an ancient time and place where Wisdom, Love and Beauty abide and the child is alive and well.

Blessed Journey,

Bonney Grey

John Grey, PhD & Bonney Grey, R.N.
co-authored *Becoming Soulmates*

They are counselors dedicated to helping
singles and couples find happiness in love.

Acknowledgements

Over the years many people have contributed to this publication, so I would like to create this opportunity to thank everyone in general who read and provided their thoughts, critical eyes, suggestions or comments as I have found everyone of them valuable. There were so many, that I am afraid I will miss some, but let me say that I most assuredly appreciate your input. First I would like to thank Ted Ryan, who first encouraged me to put the illustrations and story together in a format that others could view. He always supported every artistic endeavor that drove me to externalize my spirituality and my art. He taught me to see all of the creatures that inhabit this earth in a new and different way. Every living thing was interesting to behold, and it was always a thrill and adventure to see life from the perspective of his unique world view.

Next, my daughter Dina and her husband Jeff read my book for content, critiquing each unit, and encouraging me all the way. Dina labored over the text, editing as needed and advising on various methods of publishing formats. Also adding an editor's eye was John Pilger, a good friend and colleague who was the inspiration for several characters in the little communities and the spiritual energy that drove the essence of some of the work. He encouraged me to continue to paint and explore myself in this way. He was the portal that allowed illumination to enter, the mirror that reflected perfect insight, and the chariot that revealed the elasticity of time.

In addition, I would like to thank Ric Giardina, speaker, author of the Balanced Life series, and president of the company Spirit Employed for his encouragement and timely suggestions. Bonney & John Grey, who wrote the inspirational book, *Becoming Soulmates*, reviewed and offered important suggestions on lucidity. Bonney's insight led to an additional page and painting that brought much more clarity to the work – many thanks, Bonney.

I could not have completed this work without the assistance of Amy Vance, my administrative support staff who spent untold hours, reading, scanning illustrations, printing drafts and all of the many details of getting a book ready to go to print. Generating much enthusiasm and pointing me in the direction of a great printer, was colleague Shirley Sarraga. She is without a doubt one of the most passionately interested of my friends, and encouraged me enthusiastically as she directed me to the right people who could make this book happen. Then, adding her own creative talent, Lorna Johnson, *The Magic Font Lady*, chose just the right fonts to make the book harmonious and beautiful. Her cover design, colors, and choice of fonts are superb. Spacing of type and an eye for detail completed the package. Last, but certainly not least, I want to thank Robert Mitchell for encouraging me to put the units together into one book. His ability to see the finished product and insight into the big picture was compelling. He has repeatedly encouraged me to display my art and publish this work.

Searching for the Waters of Antiquity

Introduction

Cloaked in a charming tale of discovery, *Searching for the Waters of Antiquity* is a trilogy that takes the reader on a journey to the center of self to celebrate the Ceremony of Change. This is a place where peace, purity, and an ancient knowledge of the mysteries of life reside, where we are able to cleanse the spirit and unfold into another realm of existence. Here the protagonist finds himself walking the path of his ancestors towards the unknown, where he must choose between an ordinary life of existence or a more closely examined lifestyle. The journey begins on a desolate plane of reality and traces the process of transformation through several levels of meditation and into a new sense of awareness.

Part one of the journey finds our hero facing some of the typical anxieties befalling this level of being, and he must make choices in which there is no turning back. Leaving behind the reassurance of a sustained lifestyle, he embarks on an odyssey that takes him through two gardens of meditation. The first garden meets all of his superficial needs, while the second introduces him to the ancient waters of antiquity, which feeds his soul.

Within the second garden he finds the ancient waters of his ancestors. During this exploration he discovers an amazing temple within the mist of time that answers his questions about the four great desires of mankind. This part of the journey metaphorically explores these great desires. Encouraged by his teacher and numerous other characters that he meets along the way, he learns many lessons and presses against his boundaries, taking him even deeper into the realms of his inner life.

The protagonist must weather various trials and experiences along the way, making choices that stretch him, illuminating all that he is within his inner world. The process integrates him further and makes it possible to see life from a different perspective. This culminates in a vision of the future, seen through a light that is so beautiful that he is inspired to return to the world above to share the mysteries from beyond this world.

Part I

Beyond the Great Barrier

The Ceremony of the Change was an important part of the developmental path that lay ahead. He knew that each step counted.

Nothing could be skipped along the way. So, there he was in the middle of his journey, stuck between two worlds, unable to move in any direction. He had been successful in finding the Ancient Waters and the center of Self, for that he was grateful. But the last two rooms escaped him...

He sat in a numb stupor surveying the beauty all around him. Life went on in the enchanting little garden. The inhabitants lived their lives as they always did, chattering back and forth with benign interest in the daily mechanics of life. "All was as it should be," he lectured himself, trying to find the power inside to take the next step.

He looked deep into the pitch-black water of the pond that held so many mysteries. The reflection he saw betrayed him. He knew that the next step was not a simple one, even though it seemed so on the surface. He cleared his mind as he always did and waited for his familiar leap of faith that was always spontaneously driven by pure will. What kept him from moving? Surely the first half of the journey was the toughest, was it not? He thought so, but now he was not certain.

He looked again at his reflection knowing it would tell him nothing, but hoping against hope that the sheer will of his need would provide an answer. He wanted to move on, get through this thing, but nothing happened. He could not make himself take the next step into the unknown. He looked to his friends, but they seemed oblivious to his struggles. Somehow he could not say what was in his heart to anyone. He knew without a gesture towards even one of them that they could not help. Tension filled the air and he longed to find his teacher, but he sensed without asking that this time he was utterly on his own. Even the Source of All Things seemed inaccessible, and that was inconceivable to him.

He gave some thought to the long, arduous journey that brought him this far. He had learned many things and accomplished many trials during these days, months or had it been years? He wasn't sure, but he knew that the early times were barren of any kind of comfort. So, even though he seemed marooned between these four universal trials, he was sure it was better than the first part of the journey. He shook slightly as his memory traced back to the day he found the great cave…

He had traveled for a very long time through this strange and forbidding land. Many had made the journey before him, and he knew instinctively that it was the right thing to do.

Hunger kept him moving through the hot, dry, dusty world that he had begun to accept as home. Movement caught his eye, and he stretched as far as he could to reach a lone grub between the rocks.

As he moved on, the dust became hard, compact and darker. Or, was it the gloom of his thoughts? The ground grew hotter than even he was comfortable bearing. Here and there, black goo oozed out from the ground. White punctuated the dark rock he crossed. Noises kept him ever alert and cautious. Suddenly, a growling, roaring beast bore down on him. Stopping, he tucked himself inward and waited. Fearful yet courageous, he continued, pressed by the urge to join the others.

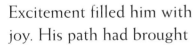

*T*hen, on one unusually hot day, his senses were startled by something he could not define. He must be close to where he was supposed to be. The others had moved on ahead of him long ago. Instinctively, he had followed their path, but to where he did not know. He only knew that he was close, very close indeed…What was that? He stopped and looked from side to side.

Excitement filled him with joy. His path had brought him forward slowly, but surely to this moment. Yes, the others had definitely been here. Passed this very spot. He stretched his neck out as far as it would go. "Yes, yes indeed, I am on the right path! But I am so very tired," he thought, "perhaps the final part of the journey can wait for the morning. I'll take shelter for the night." The hard black surface turned gray as he reached the mouth of the giant cave where he decided to rest for the night. "Rest is what I need," he thought, "just a little time to get my bearings." He tucked himself into a sound sleep.

$\mathcal{M}$orning came with a lightening jolt that scared the life out of him. The roar was so loud he felt he would never be quite the same. A huge beast laying at rest beside him made a horrible, thundering noise that very nearly took his breath away.

Then in an instant the beast was gone, and the cave shut its large mouth trapping him inside. He sat in the hot, dark stillness for what seemed like forever, daring not to move. What if the beast returned? Would it devour him with one big gulp?

Slowly he eased his head out where he might inspect the situation. Stretching his head high, he looked from side to side seeing nothing in the darkness except a lone spider crawling along, paying him no attention at all.

"Sir," he inquired rather tentatively, not knowing what kind of response he might receive. "Do you know where we are?" Nothing. "Ahem, sir," he repeated, "What kind of world is this?" Not a word would the spider reply. "Well," he thought, "He certainly isn't very friendly."

He looked around a little more, but try as he might he could not move. He seemed frozen to that very spot. "What if the beast returns," he thought. "I should not move, perhaps I should wait here for a while." As he crouched in the darkness, hungry, hot and frightened, he thought about the others that made the crossing with him. Had they safely made it to their destination?

As frightened as he was, he had the presence of mind to know he was still on the path, and going in the right direction. He mused at the notion of getting home, to the beginning, the Source of All Things. He sensed its closeness and this comforted him very much. He closed his eyes and thought he might take a nap. He felt somewhat dizzy as wave upon wave of darkness engulfed him.

Suddenly a roaring noise made him bolt forward. "What was that flash of light flooding the big cave? A crack of thunder, lightening? No? What then?" He looked from side to side.

His heart beat wildly and the terror that enveloped him was replaced by a burst of energy. He ran like he never had before.

Heart pounding, he felt himself lifted high in the air. "What had him" betrayed by his body, he was suspended in space high in the mouth of the cave. Body fluid poured from him as anxiety overtook him.

A huge creature held him up, peering at him, his withered legs dangling and his head tucked tightly to his body. "What will become of me," he thought?

The creature extended him at arm's length and examined him carefully. "He's dehydrated," she thought to herself, "close to death. I wonder how long he has been trapped in here?"

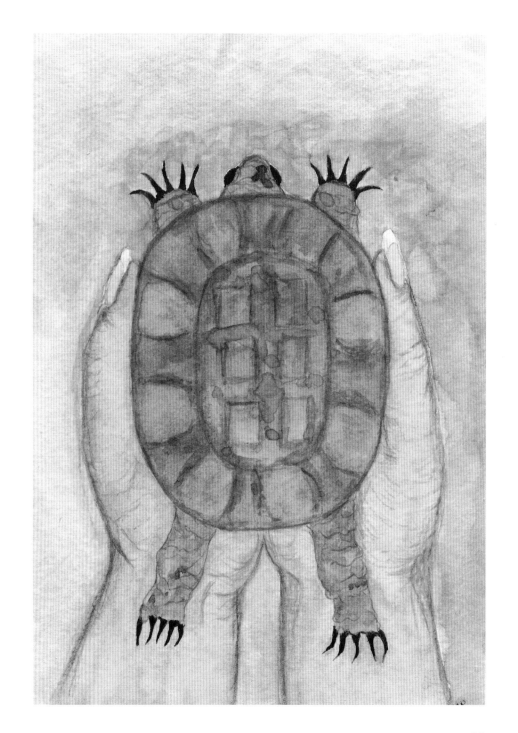

He was transported through a maze of light and dark. Shiny things sparkled here and there as the giant carried him into the back of the cave and out to a beautiful world.

She set him in a clump of viola leaves, in a cool, damp green spot in the middle of her garden. And then she was gone, just like that!

He sat motionless for a long time, waiting for something to happen. He saw movement here and there, watching eyes assessing his progress.

Soon he realized nothing would hurt him here and he looked around the wonderland in awe. Never had he experienced anything like this.

"Wow" he thought, "wait until I tell the others. But now, I just have to rest." He walked slowly through the cool damp garden. Grubs all over the place, he thought, munching here and there. He took a deep long breath, found a place to be still and soon he was fast asleep.

The leaves rustled in the early morning breeze. He looked from side to side as light illuminated his world. "It's morning," he thought, "and I am alive. I am still on my path and there is food every where! More importantly, I did not die! I cannot wait to tell the others about the great beast, the she-creature and this beautiful place."

Then a great noise swooshed through the big garden. Huge black spikes lifted up through the ground, and along with it, a torrent of water sprayed hard on everything in sight. He stood still not knowing what to expect. The noise was terrifying, but the water felt good. Stretching his neck out he let the water spray him all over for what seemed like a long time.

The rains usually did not fall at this time of the year. He felt as though he had been given a special gift from above. As he savored the moment, he did not realize that he would be so blessed every single day at that precise moment.

He wandered around the leaves, bushes and flowers picking up grubs as he went. He explored the grounds very carefully in the next few days. As he did, the tall gray barrier blocking his path always stopped him.

One day he followed the barrier for what seemed like forever, never finding anything but more gray barriers blocking his way. "Well," he thought, "Maybe I am here! Maybe this is my destiny?" His mind whirled as he thought and thought. But deep down he knew he really wasn't where he was supposed to be. He looked around and assessed his surroundings. What a beautiful place, and there was plenty to eat. He breathed a big sigh and settled in for another night wondering how he would get on his path again.

After days of exploring, the ground became very hard again. "Oh," he thought, "this is like the place before the cave." Hard gray ground. He moved cautiously across the ground until he bumped into two big, round, stringy things. He froze as the hairy creatures made noises he didn't understand, and were gone as suddenly as they had appeared. He sighed softly from relief and tried to get his bearings again.

$\mathscr{N}$ow," he thought, "What was I doing?" Before he could get himself back on track, the big hairy ones were back. This time he saw that they were connected to a very huge creature. The creature dropped little brown pebbles down beside him. He froze again, tucking his head deep inside, terrified to move. Then something extraordinary happened. He looked at the pebbles with one eye open. "That smells like something to eat," he thought excitedly. "I have never smelled that before, but I am sure it is something to eat."

$\mathcal{D}$are I try a taste?" He looked up at the creature. The creature sat patiently waiting for something.

"Perhaps he means for me to eat it," he thought suspiciously. "Maybe it is a trick! Well, there is only one way to find out." He stretched his neck out and reached for one of the small brown pebbles. He tried and he tried to break the morsel so that he might eat some. "It is very hard, but tasty," he thought, "tasty indeed."

"Well worth the effort, I have never tasted anything like this." He took his time and ate more of the little pebbles. From time to time he looked at the big creature that seemed to enjoy watching him.

Out of the corner of his eye he saw them closing in from the rear. Frightening swirls of stringing hair swooping down upon him, eating up his pebbles and sniffing him all over. He just sat petrified, tucked his head in, closed his eyes shut very tight and did not move. The huge creature took the hairy ones by the neck, voice booming, he said, "HEY, LEAVE THE LITTLE GUY ALONE!" Huh? "Yes, that is me, I am the little guy the creature is talking about!"

Well, no one ever stood up for him before, especially not a huge creature like this one. He felt very special, very special indeed. He wondered what the others would say if they knew! The creature looked down on the little guy and said, "Hmmm, I am glad you joined our garden, it's a pleasure to have you here." Then the other one that brought him originally to the garden joined him. "Wow, I can't believe he survived!" she said somewhat surprised. "With that kind of spunk he deserves a name." "A name?" he repeated. The big creature smiled, knowing his partner was like that. "What do you have in mind?" he said. "Oh, I don't know yet, something will come up..."

Every morning the little guy came out of the hosta leaves where he had made a temporary home close to the patio. There he would find five or six little brown pebbles. Even though there was always plenty to eat in the beautiful garden, the little brown pebbles were a wonderful treat given by the huge creatures. He began to look forward to these treats and came to the patio daily in search of the morsels.

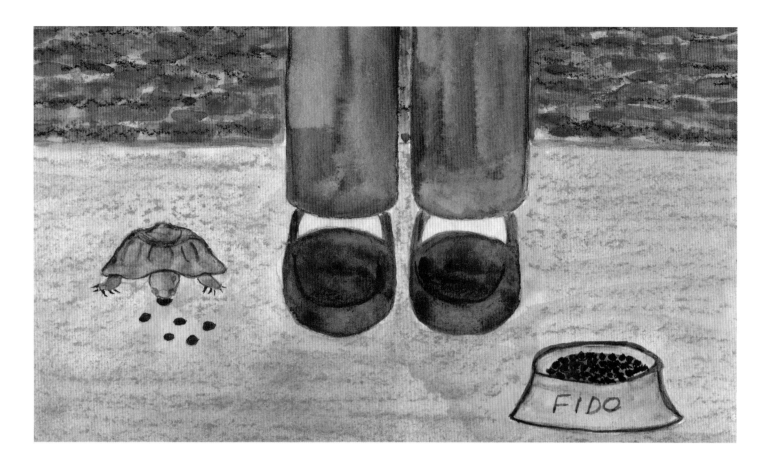

As time went on, even the hairy ones seemed to accept his presence offering only a casual sniff as they explored the patio. The longhaired gray one always intrigued him. Though try as he might, he could not get his attention. He followed him around hoping to find out what he knew about what was beyond the great barrier. Word was that the little gray one had been past the barrier to the beyond, which he felt sure, had something to do with his path.

The huge creatures watched the long gray hairy one and the little guy tagging along after him. What a priceless sight, she smiled to herself. "He tags along like a baby following his momma," she said to the bigger of the two creatures. "Let's call him Tag," she said. The huge creature smiled then too, and said "That sounds fitting, Tag it is." They watched as Tag meandered into the hosta leaves.

$\mathcal{E}$xploring became a favorite pastime for Tag. He moved in and out of the vegetation with agility, betraying his hard exterior. Tag moved up and down small mounds, through the paths, around rock clusters and trees. He was intimately acquainted with the other inhabitants of the garden: The mouse that lived under the lilac bush with her brood of youngsters, the fish in the ponds and a multitude of birds of every color. Red ones, blue ones, little yellow ones and the tiniest one that hummed around the pink flowers. He was very comfortable in the garden feeling as much at home as he had been anywhere. There was plenty of food and always the little brown pebbles for treats. The little garden was in complete harmony.

One day, Tag was between the willow and the big rock munching grubs when he spotted a familiar sight. He stopped in his tracks and tucked his head tight within himself. He was unsure whether to be excited or cautious. There before him were two more of him, only bigger.

Tag stretched his neck out and peered carefully at the two newcomers. "Where did you guys come from?" he inquired.

The oldest and biggest of the two stretched his long neck toward Tag and groaned,

"Who's asking?" "It is me, Tag," he exclaimed with wide eyed anticipation. "The great creatures gave me my name." "Well, Tag, we are passing through on our way to the ancient waters. Are you not going to the place of our ancestors, my son?" His gnarly voice reminded him of some of the old ones of his clan. Tag felt a stab of pain as he remembered the others and their journey to the ancient waters.

*H*e looked into the old one's eyes and asked him when he was going to the place of his ancestors. He peered at Tag intently. "Well son, we pass through this garden each year to rest, and usually stay a few weeks. Nice place, huh, son?" "Yes it is," said Tag as he surveyed the beautiful little garden. Tag sighed, "I guess I thought this was the ancient place. It seems so special." The old one looked at the traveling companion. She spoke, "An easy mistake to make my son. However, this is merely a stopping place on the way of your path. Our first year we stayed through the flowering time and the coloring of the leaves. We almost stayed too long. Make sure to be on your way in time for the Ceremony of the Change." "I will," replied Tag. He looked again at the beautiful garden, sighing audibly.

*T*ime passed, and the two visitors were rested and prepared for the last leg of their journey. The old one moved closer to Tag, and spoke, "The time has come to join the others, would you not like to travel with us?" Tag reflected a moment, he knew the old ones would be the best guide to the beyond. They knew even more than the gray, stringy one about the journey. But, even though it made sense, he could not go just yet. "Gee, no thank you sir, I want to stay as long as I can with my new friends," he said. The great creatures and the hairy ones had become very dear to him. And Tag had really come to love the little brown pebbles as well. He would stay a bit longer and wander through the trails and up the mounds.

Tag munched a little brown pebble marveling over the taste. He had never tasted anything like this exquisite flavor before. Just then he felt a thud on his head. Looking up he noticed many things falling from the trees. First the little brown things that some of the inhabitants of the garden really liked to eat. Then, there were the yellow, orange and brown things fluttering in the breeze. As he looked around he recognized the signs of the big change and a great fright moved through him.

He remembered the old one's warning. Moving through the garden, he knew he had to choose. Soon he would be stuck here during the danger time without the aid of the others.

*H*e looked around the beautiful garden and felt very confused. He wanted both to stay and go, but that was impossible. Time was growing short and the days grew cold. Tag went to the place where the little brown pebbles were laid every day. He tried to eat but could not. He stepped over them and wandered toward the tall barrier that stood between the great beyond and the garden. The old ones had shown him the way through the barrier. Two mouse holes stood side by side next to the water that fell from the rocks. He looked back at the hairy ones who like to play at the top of the mounds. He would miss the one with long gray hair. The great creatures had not been around for some time. Just as well, he decided. It would be much harder to say good-bye.

*T*ag looked through the mouse hole toward the massive beyond ahead. He was instantly excited at the prospect of joining the others. His excitement turned briefly to anxiety as he realized the enormity of what laid ahead. Just when he felt the most afraid, he heard the old one groan, "It is time to be with the others Tag, come along to the ancient waters for the Ceremony of the Change."

Tag blinked and moved his head from side to side. "What was that? Did anyone else hear anything?" Tag cleared his throat and took a deep breath. "Oh well…" Tag moved through the mouse hole and into the great beyond. The unknown loomed in front of him as he stepped through the tall grasses on his way to the ceremony of the winter solstice. The time had come to share in the joy of this beautiful tradition and he knew he earned his place with the others. Tag meandered through the tall grasses, "I wonder what new adventures await me past the Great Beyond?"

Epilogue

Tag weighed carefully the decision to continue the journey and examine the mysteries of the ancient world of antiquity. Life in the little garden fulfilled all of his physical and emotional needs, but the ancient call intrigued him. Torn between two worlds, he was compelled to continue towards the unknown. Moving forward was a life decision that both frightened and exhilarated him. This journey, when approached from fear and doubt, can be a disturbing one. At some point he had to move past the fear that kept him stuck, and find a way to *see* that was nourishing to himself and to others.

This is the journey of integration that connects the culture and traditions of the physical world, with the fabric of the Universe. The journey that we cannot fail, but insists that we see with clarity into the depth and center of Self. That said, how does Tag get unstuck? Where does the ancient journey take him? How does he move past the mechanics of living and evolve the spiritual side of the personality? This is a decision that involves strength, determination and dedication to gentle self-examination.

Blessings of the fruits of his labor freed him to investigate the essence of being fully alive. The exploration of who we are at the very depth of being and how our connections with self and others help us to evolve, is the ancient work of the spirit.

So, what does it take to make the next move towards fulfilling the need to balance the personality, with the incomprehensible fabric of the soul? How do we want to be remembered and what can we contribute to the unfolding of humanity? This is the evolution of life, the work of the individual and collective soul. This is both the challenge and love of our lives here on this planet called Earth, a school for the ongoing development of humanity.

Part II

Tag's Magnificent Journey

$\mathcal{T}$ag walked and walked through the tall grasses in the cold driving rain. Indeed, he had waited too long to begin his journey. The old ones and some of the other inhabitants in the creature's garden had warned him that the winters were harsh around here. The days turned dark and white stuff floated through the air, creating a bitter cold that Tag had never experienced. He was usually safe asleep by now with the others, tucked in small dark holes all snug for the winter solstice. "At least there are no predators to get me. No one in their right mind would be out in this stuff," he thought. He looked around the terrain. He saw nothing familiar, but he knew he was going in the right direction.

After many days, Tag walked through the grasses into a stand of tall and majestic trees. In the middle of the darkness was a bath of sunlight. "Oh look," he thought to himself, "I'll bet it is warmer over there."

He walked quickly to the sunlit area and stood for a long time, bathing in warmth and a sense of calm and safety. As he stood there, comfortable at last, he felt a strong urge to turn around. "Was that there before?" he asked himself. There in front of him was another path that again was filled with streams of light that made the bushes and trees shimmer with brilliant hues of green.

Tag was intrigued by his find and decided to follow the path to see where it went. As he moved forward the path descended deep into a clearing. No, look, he thought as he maneuvered the bend in the path, "Oh my, a spectacular garden!" He studied the area intently, "This garden is even more beautiful than the one that belonged to the friendly creatures."

He was taken with the beauty of the place as he stepped down where he could see more. Below him were mighty trees and blossoming bushes and a beautiful pond with a waterfall fed by an unseen source. The waterfall beat a constant rhythm and the multitude of colorful birds hummed a beautiful mystical melody. Butterflies kept in tune, moving from flower to flower in time with the music. Winter seemed to have forgotten this peaceful place – which languished in full spring.

He was beside himself with pure joy. "I have arrived, I am sure of it!" This must be the ancient water he was looking for, the place of his ancestors that he had traveled so far to find…he had arrived, indeed!

The garden was tucked deep into a gully, surrounded by high walls of earth, dotted with trees and bushes. He stepped down the steep path, which gradually descended into the lovely garden. He kept his eyes on the path, fearful he would lose his footing. About half way he stopped to look down into the water below.

*T*ag was stunned by what he saw. There in the water's reflection floating dreamily was the bluest sky punctuated by fluffy white clouds. He looked up through the trees, seeing nothing above but darkness. It was nighttime when he arrived here, he reminded himself. He looked down again and gasped. In the middle of the sky and clouds was a beautiful…What was it? A castle perhaps, or some kind of beautiful kingdom. A temple, he thought, yes a temple!

He was both intrigued and anxious. He stood there for a long moment wondering if he should go further into the garden or run from the images that unsettled him so much. He pulled himself up high and proud, breathing deeply. He would not run. He came looking for the water. It was his responsibility to find it and go through the Ceremony of the Change as his fathers before him. He was determined that he would not fail in this as some of the others before him.

Tag took a breath and stepped down again and again, following the path until he had descended to the floor of the garden.

$\mathcal{T}$he path had led him to the water's edge. He stood still, blinking, hoping to escape the building anxiety. What was he supposed to do now? "I am a land turtle," he thought, "I cannot swim, can I?" He wondered what to do next. The water turned pitch black and looked very deep. As he tried to get his balance the water began to shimmer. There to his amazement the water became cerulean blue again with floating billowy clouds spotted here and there. He took a step back and gasped. What did it mean? It didn't look like a reflection at all. It looked more like a sky…albeit a surreal, mystical sky. "What do I do now? If I jump, either way I fall or drown." His heart thumped wildly as he stood there trying to orient himself to his fate.

Then he heard a soft and melodic voice from somewhere within the garden, "Feel the truth of your decision, Tag." He knew the answer before it was told to him. "No harm will come to those who, in good faith, walk their rightful path." He looked up to see a rather stately bird with delicate colorful feathers. She seemed to have the answer to everything in her warm, friendly eyes. He nodded a knowing glance, took a deep breath and dramatically *leaped* out into the unknown....

Instead of falling or drowning, Tag settled gently on firm ground. He looked beneath himself and from side to side, and then up above, but saw nothing but blue sky and clouds. He stood still wondering what to do next, then urged on by instinct he took a few steps through a cloud. As his vision cleared, he saw what he was looking for – the temple that appeared in the water while descending the path to the floor of the garden.

*T*ag looked at the temple for a long while. "What is this place?" It shimmered through the clouds and sparkled with what looked like gold and jewels. "What is the *Ceremony of the Change* anyway? Some of the others called it the *Great Transformation!* What does that mean?" he thought as he took another step forward. Curiosity and a deep sense of wonder replaced his anxiety. He knew he could not turn back. Moving forward, he ascended the stairs.

*H*e made his way through the entrance into cool, semi-darkened corridors of shining walls and soft as velvet floors. In front of him was an archway with the words: *Halls of Wisdom & Knowledge,* written in gold lettering.

He stood thinking the words. "What kind of knowledge would that be?" He remembered the instincts he was born with and his mother who showed him how to do certain things to find food and such. Somehow, he knew this was different and he obediently moved through the door to the Great Hall.

Inside he found a large room with illuminated walls, in the middle of each of the four walls was an arched doorway with gold leaf letters shining above each entrance. The first door held the word *Love,* the next *Compassion,* then *Affection* and the last word spelled out *Impartiality.* These are the great desires of all that inhabit the kingdom, and those who are one with the Source of All Things will receive them in due course.

Tag looked from door to door wondering what to do next. He took a few more steps into the room and looked around a bit more. There beside each door were gems, gold shiny things and other special objects, but none so special than what he imagined were in the rooms that the doors led to. He became aware of the middle of the room. In the center were several very tall, glowing, crystal pillars.

*H*e walked forward in curiosity, his eyes tracing the crystal pillars upward to the shimmering, surreal sky sparkling with many colors, punctuated with a cloud or two here and there. He moved to the base of the pillar and looked down. There was no floor! "What was it?" he thought, "Translucent sky, or something else?" He did not have words for what the saw, and tried to use words of objects that closely resembled the images.

There was a sort of energy beneath him and all around him and he translated it to material images of worth. He sensed there was the same energy flowing through all things: the trees, the sky, the rocks, and the other animals. Especially the creatures in the first garden he stayed in and the "things" that the creatures enjoyed as well.

*T*ag stood transfixed. He did not know what to think. Then his curiosity gave way to anxiety as he looked down at his right claw. It was not where he last saw it. His whole foot was gone. His heart pumped frantically as he tried to make sense of what he was seeing, or not seeing. His anxiety turned to panic. He did not feel his shell on his back either. What was happening to him? Where was his body? He was getting light-headed with fatigue and fear.

Suddenly he heard a voice, or was it the sound of some inner knowing? He was all at once calm as he felt the words start to make sense. "Tag, nothing will harm you here. These are the *Great Halls of Antiquity* and you are meant to be here. It is part of your path's work." "Am I dead?" Tag ventured a sudden thought. "Oh no, you are very much alive, you are reality. There is no death and no separation. It is the world that is an illusion and you but play a part."

While he was confused, an ancient part of himself understood and did not question those thoughts. What he did question was what he needed to do. The answer came quickly. "Watch carefully to unlearn those things that bring you fear, guilt and separation from others. Correct yourself and move forward, but think not of these things again. This is your life's work, and in becoming free, you free all others as well." "Oh," he said, not sure he really understood. "How do 'I' free others?" he said humbly, surely that really didn't mean what it implied. "You will understand by the behavior of those freed," came the simple answer.

*T*ag looked around him at the doors to the rooms that conveyed so much: the doors of *Love, Compassion, Affection,* and *Impartiality.* "Do not concern yourself. What you need to know will come to you at the time that you need to know. No plan is needed, Tag. Listen well and the knowledge you need will come to you from the Great Source of All Things, for which we are all connected.

He thought about this for some time and then he knew what was asked of him. Simply to be happy and to put himself in situations that bring him peace. Then he would be able to give to all he meets a sense of peace, joy and love. For how could one be truly happy while giving his brothers anything other than this? He closed his eyes and smiled from an inner knowing.

*A*t this thought Tag felt a great whoosh, which dazed him, making him feel off kilter. He opened his eyes and tried to get his bearing again. "Wait a minute," he thought. "He was in the very place he stood when he made the first step towards the clouds."

He stood looking at the pitch-black pond before him. He hadn't moved an inch, or had he? Well, this was a strange journey indeed. What had he learned? Who had spoken to him? Was it the Old Ones, the Universe, or was it God? Allah? Buddha? Muhammad?

Or perhaps something else had provided him with this knowledge?"

Whoever had spoken to him, Tag understood something very well from his journey. All paths lead to the same place and only one place, the Source of All Things. He understood that great knowledge was given to everyone equally, but interpreted a bit differently from land to land. Each creature used their experiences to tell their story to their descendents in their own special way.

And the rooms, I wonder what's in the rooms of all great desires? Well, I can't wait to tell everyone I meet, but who would believe a tale so strange as this?" he mused as he wandered the garden, waiting for spring to come to the land above him. "But I'll try," he thought smiling to himself. "Indeed I will!"

Epilogue

When the joy of the moment passed and Tag was able to think things through, he watched the water for a long while, until he was very tired. There was so much that was spinning around in his head from all that he experienced in the little garden, and especially the magic temple. There he understood the unfolding of life with such clarity that he was stunned by the simple truth.

The subjective fantasy, with its constant decent into the depths of Self, opened the door to his internal garden, the garden of his soul, the temple or kingdom within. This is the place that holds all of the knowledge of the Universe, if you have the courage to persist. Would he? He did not know. Everything was jumbled and running around in place. Did he have the dedication and self trust that he needed to fearlessly look within?

More importantly, did he trust the Universe to provide all that he needed to do so? Tag knew that whatever he needed would be granted him, if he walked his rightful path. He knew that he could learn to listen to his internal teacher, the wisdom within the center of Self and the right path would be illuminated before him. This is the work of the soul, to learn to see with nonphysical eyes the path before you, to sense and feel the energy that aligns the soul with man's hearts desires. Here we explore the path of Love, Compassion, and Affection in a way that is detached, with Impartiality and that is what drives the spirit towards fulfillment.

Tag hesitated. Unlearn what brings you guilt and fear? Is that possible? However would our world function without it? He tried to feel the essence of the message. Somewhere in his heart he knew the truth. That we cannot hold two experiences concurrently. We cannot love and fear at the same time, so he would have to elevate himself through fear and into the light, into love. Which would it be? He was told clearly and succinctly that doing so would free the Self and all others as well. The pressure of the moment froze him in time, but somewhere within, he found the courage to step onto the path that led back to the temple with grace and dignity. He would not surrender to the urge to bolt. He would continue towards the path of the unknown. This is the strength given to him from the Source of All Things. He could not fail.

Part III

Waiting for Spring

Exploring the mysterious and enchanted little garden became Tag's full time job. Many creatures of all shapes, sizes and colors came and went around him, and he became a great friend to them all. He was continually amazed that just above him a blustery winter wailed, while he felt safe and warm in this protected space. He was completely happy and at peace waiting for spring.

Once and a while he would make his way to the temple to visit the Great Hall of Antiquity and would speak to the Source of All Things. During all of this time he never asked about the four rooms that surrounded the Great Hall. Somehow he knew that eventually he would want to go there. Really, who would not want to see them? Combined they made up all the universal desires of mankind.

There's great wisdom stored in dose rooms," the old jay told him one day, "and all dat go dere are richly rewarded," he drawled with some kind of accent Tag could not define. "Have you been there?" Tag inquired excitedly. "Well no," replied the jay, clearing his throat. "I'm too old ta make dat journey," he fibbed, fluttering nervously. "Lots of folk say dey been, but I don't tink dey really been, Tag," he said knowingly. "Cause, dere's a kind of peace about dose dat been, ya know?" "No," Tag said, "What do you mean?" "Well, ya just know, dat's all!" "Now Ms. Crane's been, at least dat's what everybody sez, and I believes it." "Go ask her and you'll see what I mean," he said inching away from Tag.

Recovering from his breach of self, he continued to encourage Tag to make the journey. "Dey say dat each room has ta be entered in dis order: first Love, den Compassion, next Affection, and den Impartiality. Dere can be no deviation from dis rule," remarked the jay. "Oh," Tag said, "why do you think they have a rule like that?" "Well how'd I know, why don't ya ask the Source of All Things?" Seems like a more fitting question for Him. "Oh, yes I guess so…" Tag, could see that he was irritating the old jay, so he excused himself.

$\mathcal{M}$eandering down the path towards the pond he could see Ms. Crane and he moved steadily towards her. He was beginning to get more curious about the rooms that held the key to man's great desires and wanted to ask her what she knew of these things. Tag approached her and mentioned that he had heard she had been to the temple. He looked deep into Ms. Crane's eyes and asked her directly if she had entered the rooms. "Well, yes I have Tag, why do you ask?" "Well, everyone says you have been there and I have grown very curious about the rooms."

Ms. Crane looked at Tag intently for a while. Then she spoke, "Well, Tag, I could tell you about the rooms, but why don't you go and see for yourself?" Tag was taken back by the comment, not expecting the challenge. "Well," he sputtered, "I was just curious, so I thought you could tell me about it…" he trailed off, not knowing what to do next. Ms. Crane softened her voice to a caress as she began to explain her thinking to Tag. "I could tell you with words, Tag, but the rooms are to be experienced first hand. The words alone would not hold much meaning for you," she said flatly. "Really, Tag, the rewards are greater than the fear that keeps you from the experience." "Oh," he said nodding thoughtfully. "Well, I guess I have to think about it Ms. Crane," buying himself some time. She nodded back knowingly and continued on her way.

$\mathcal{T}$ag amused himself day after day talking to the creatures of the garden, but avoiding the inevitable challenge made to him. He so wanted to see for himself what was in the rooms, but he also knew that if he went, he would never be the same. This frightened him so much that he began to avoid the temple itself. Then one day he was looking at himself in the pond and realized that he could delay this challenge no longer. He could not separate himself from the Source of All Things one more moment, and to go back to the temple meant he would have to continue the journey to the rooms of transformation. That is what he came here originally to do. Visit the Waters of Antiquity and go through the Ceremony of the Change, had he not?

He made his way down the path to the dark waters of the pond and stood there before it. Then he took a deep breath and jumped into the water, emerging into the depths of antiquity. Looking intently through the mist at the temple, he started the climb up the stairs and through the Halls of Wisdom and past the Great Hall of Antiquity.

*T*ag walked down the long hall of love towards the door's entrance. As he moved closer he began to feel the familiar lightness inside that was typical of being within the temple and near the Great Hall. The weight of his shell disappeared, and he glided towards the door as if he were floating inches above the floor.

Standing motionless, he paused for a moment, then took a step towards it as he watched in stunned silence as the door opened. It was as if a magic wand was waved before it. He looked in the room and saw nothing in particular, but while it held nothing special to the eye, the light-filled room beckoned to him.

Then within the center of the room a spark of light began to flicker ever so softly, and growing stronger, the sheer energy of it drew him in. He took a step across the threshold, feeling himself transcend the doorway.

Pressing his foot downward on the floor of the room, something miraculous happened. A thousand beams of light pulsated through the center of the room splaying forth a glorious stream of energy. Magnetic and full of life, the light filled the center of the room. One more step had Tag fully engaged, and he was enveloped in the movement of light and sound. It was indefinable.

Tag stood in awe, transfixed by the moment. He took one more step, and seemed to be squarely in the middle of the room. Time stood still as he experienced what seemed like both a moment and everlasting eternity. He was overwhelmed, swallowed up by the experience. The feeling was so all encompassing that he wanted to run back through the door. He tried to move, but could not. He felt like he was losing his very soul, and wondered how he would live through it.

All four of Tag's feet were glued to the floor. He did not want to leave this beautiful experience, but was terrified of the loss that he imagined coming. He could not feel the weight of his shell that he had carried for a lifetime. He could not see the claws on his feet or the shadow of himself that usually shown in the lighted reflection on the wall. He was stunned by all that was happening to him. He looked again at his body. Where did he go? Tag questioned himself, and anyone that might be able to hear. He questioned the Source of All Things, imploring Him for some answer to what he was experiencing. This was completely foreign to him. He had never felt such feelings before, and was definitely outside the comfort of familiar territory.

Tag braced himself, took a breath and closed his eyes to physical sight, preparing to know the true essence of life itself. He was to encounter the only experience worth having. The one and only knowledge that antiquity will allow across the threshold of life to death of the physical body. He sensed an inner knowing...

Yes, you can take love with you. Yes, this experience will endure the ravages of time and space. The Universe will never deprive anyone of the will of love and its healing force. The task is to take that step across the threshold into the center of its existence. To move sure-footed into the center of the eye of the storm. Love in all its glory can never harm. Only what we think about it during the experience can harm us.

Tag felt reinforced and adjusted his footing, getting a firm stance as he watched the light move in waves through the room. He looked at the beauty unfolding with anxious interest. He could see the light's movement sway to and fro. The rhythm and movement enchanted him, creating a dance of light centered within this magnificent room.

*M*esmerized, Tag watched with growing intrigue as the light expanded into particles, then what appeared to be golden circles of light. He watched the glowing balls illuminate and float up into the air, like carbonated fluid splaying into the center of the room.

Filled with a magnetic softness, he was riveted to the spot. He could not move, but now he did not want to. He was deliriously happy, and terrified at the same time. Terrified of the feeling of being overwhelmed by a force he could not control. The only recourse to him was to stay. He was drawn to the center of the room like a moth to the flame. Caught in a spider's web of feeling, he was immobilized at the center of timelessness itself.

Completely immersed, he was struck by the beauty of all that was happening. Letting go meant separating himself from his belief of control. He felt vulnerable in the face of utter danger. Tag could do nothing but breathe in the experience of this moment.

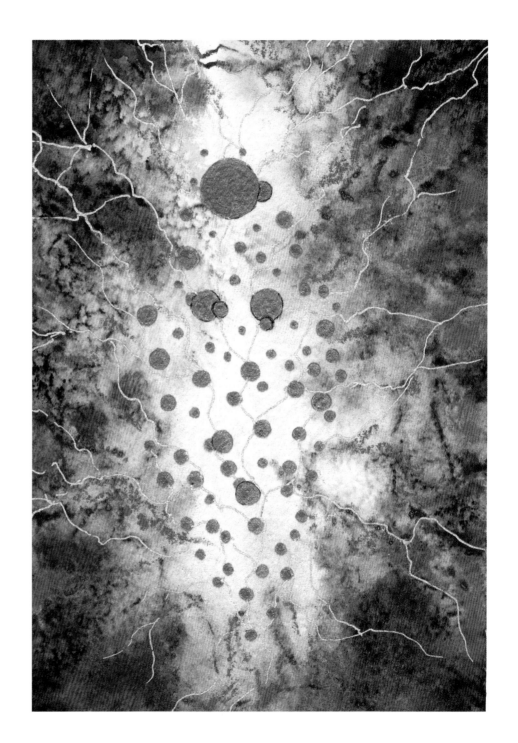

*T*ag strained forward towards two of the glowing circles of light, resonating as they expanded and grew to equal size, meeting each other at the center of the room. He knew at that moment that he was one of those glowing circles. Observing the circles as they moved together, they pulsated and touched only slightly. Then with more determination, the circles met, overlapping in a burst of will. Covering a mere fraction of each other, it felt like an all-encompassing enveloping of the soul within the circle of life.

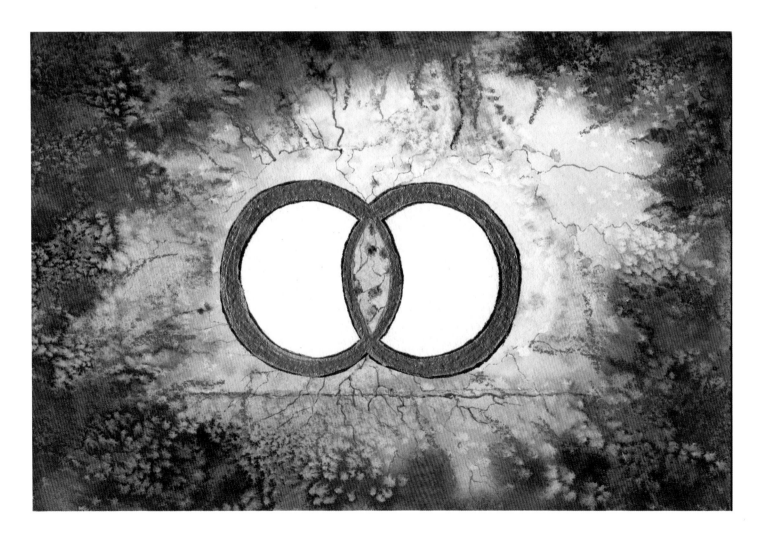

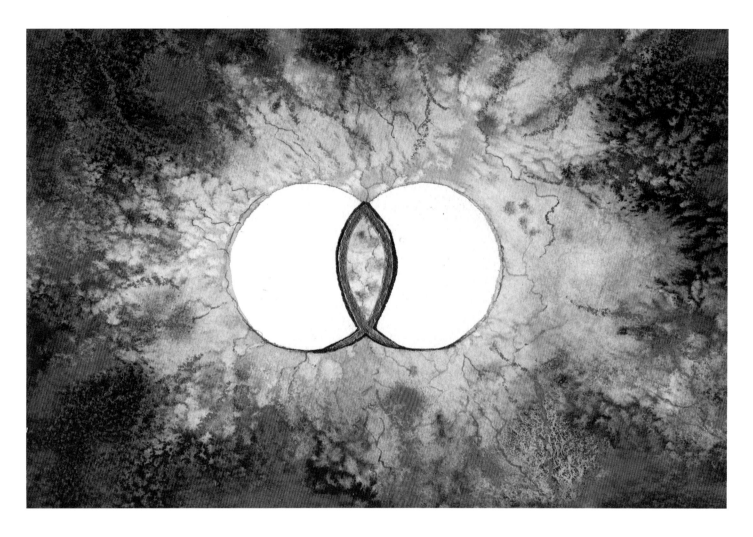

*E*ach circle tried to pull away to remove itself from the sheer beauty and presence of the other. But not able to let go, the two stayed and fought the engulfing terror of the unknown. Then the inconceivable happened. For a few magical moments, the circles disappeared and the center of the combined circle remained.

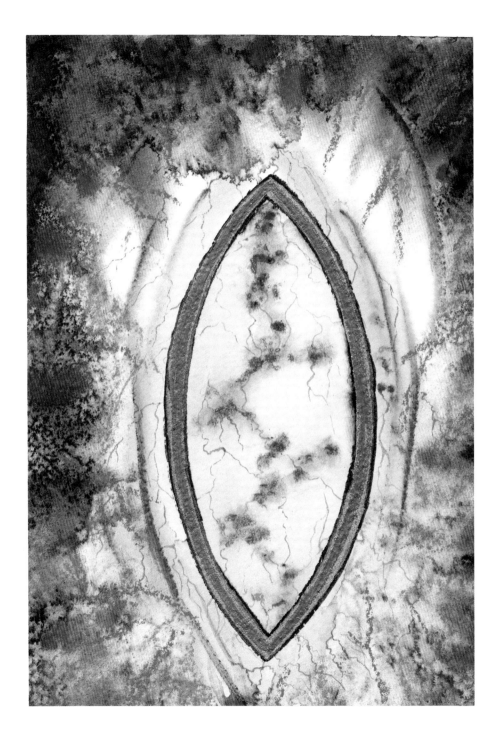

The almond-shaped form stayed in the room of love, and a third entity from the original circles evolved. The center of the two circles united, were more than the two that formed itself. The mandorla illuminated brightly resonating with truth. Combined they revealed an inner beauty that was so radiant that time and space was irrelevant.

All else ceased to exist, and fully engaged in the center of love it completed itself in sublime, esoteric wonder.

*T*ag's head was spinning, confused, he could watch no more. The rules and structure of life, the physics that regulated the room's equilibrium was temporarily suspended. He wanted very much to stay in the moment where transformation would carry him to another plane of existence. He knew this to be true, and remembered all of the times that he overlapped with the other creatures in the beautiful little garden. Those were sweet memories of moments spent in shared experience like the circles united here in full abandon. While he knew that all creatures can experience this phenomenon together in platonic meetings of higher self, he also knew that sometimes a special experience stands out from all the rest.

He tried to control his deep, passionate sense of the moment to keep it from overwhelming. He tried again to move. Possessed by the experience, he desperately needed to get away from the raw emotion that gripped him, restraining his every movement. He had felt a vague memory of this, but could not place where he experienced it. Then instantly he knew that it was a memory from another time, a time from beyond this world, a time at the depths of antiquity. The beauty was too much to behold and he felt a sudden strong urge to bolt.

Tag recognized in a moment that all experiences that attract two circles of light together are love based which is at the core of existence. Only thought relegates the experience to anything low or base such as found in fear. At that moment, a surge of fear broke the spell of love's beauty, and Tag sensed he could move. Reluctantly, he made his body ambulate toward the door, stepping over the threshold to his utter dismay, into the sameness and ordinariness of life alone. As he made his way back to the garden he sensed the feelings slipping away. The miracle of the moment was passing into the history of his memory and he grieved deeply for the lost dream, a trace of memory still etched on his heart of hearts.

Tag moved down the hall of love, saddened by the loss of that experience which he feared would never be his again. Then he felt a presence that usually only came in the Great Halls of Antiquity. The Source of All things clearly and succinctly articulated the following.

Every circle is equal in my eyes. All have equal light and all are one with me. Each circle of light illuminates with full radiance and each creature possesses the ability to unite, enveloping and overlapping to form the essence of love. When the circles remove their superfluous self, what remains is pure love. The almond-shaped center represents the existence of purity itself. This purity is without pretense and has the ability to cross all boundaries and all relationships. Only conditioned thought protects us from the experience of eternal and timeless beauty.

Tag thought tenderly about what he knew to be a great truth. Confused, he was both anxious and reluctant to leave. Moving slowly down the hall, he made his way towards the entrance of the temple, down the steps and into the mist of time. A familiar whoosh and he was back at the water's edge, unsure that he had moved at all. Although he was relieved to be back, he was also saddened at what he left behind.

The days were unending as he tried to resume his usual life. He talked to the same creatures of the garden as he always did, and though he cared about them, he found little amusement in the typical banter they engaged in.

As the days came and went Tag began to feel better, gradually forgetting the loss as he tried to remember the beauty of the experience. "But what had he learned?" He quizzed himself repeatedly. "Wasn't that the reason he came to the garden in the first place, to experience the transformation? What about the next room, and when would he go back? Could he go back?" He did not know.

*H*e struggled with these thoughts until he was very tired and completely confused. Then one day he went to see if he could find Ms. Crane. She always helped him when he could not figure things out. He looked and he looked, but he could not find her. He asked the other creatures of the garden, but it had been a while since anyone had seen her. He was becoming frightened for her safety, when there she was in front of him. He did not know how she got there. He must have been very preoccupied not to see her move towards him, but he was glad that she was there. He did so appreciate her wisdom in such things.

Ms. Crane looked at him with her dark brown eyes that bore right through to the very depths of him. She waited patiently for him to speak, but he did not know what to say. Then he began simply to tell her what he experienced in the Room of Love. She waited until he had given her every detail that he could remember.

When he paused, she smiled at him with the warmth of a million candles.

*H*e immediately felt better, because he knew instantly that she had really been to all of the rooms and would help him get through whatever he was going through.

He waited for her to speak. When she did, he was completely unnerved. "Tag," she inquired, "What made you leave the room?" "Well, I, I don't know," he stammered searching for something to say that she would accept as reasonable. "I was afraid I guess," he offered. "Hmmm"…she purred at him, just a little soft smile forming in the corner of her eyes and mouth. "Afraid of what?" she persisted. "Well, I am not sure," he looked down at the ground trying to think what had him so gripped in terror. The very thought of it made him queasy as he remembered the moments before he bolted for the door.

Try as he might, he could offer no explanation for his reaction to beauty in its purist form. Tag made several suggestions that even he couldn't accept. Ms. Crane looked at him, amusement tickling the corners of her mouth. He was completely frustrated, because he knew that she knew the answer already, but would not tell him why he reacted in the way that he did.

Then in that moment he knew, and he couldn't believe his own thoughts. He could not stay because it would mean a change in the fundamental way that he thought about things. His entire belief system would have to adjust to accommodate this new view of life and adapt to behold the wonder of the Universe. He would have to see the flip side of things and in doing so he would truly be happy at the depth of himself. This was completely foreign to his style. The more he thought how he eloped from the room, the guiltier and sadder he felt. How could he do this to himself? After all, he was a good turtle and deserved the best of things.

Ms. Crane stood watching Tag grow sadder by the moment. She smiled a compassionate smile that seemed to hold the knowledge of the Universe. "Tag, you have learned your lesson well, and you can re-enter the room at any time." Her soothing voice seemed to heal him at the very depth of his soul. "Now is the time to absorb energy from all of your resources. Understand what keeps you from accepting all of the beauty that you deserve. When you are ready, you can go back to the room." Tag stood before her basking in her warmth. He was so very grateful for Ms. Crane's insight; he smiled at her with new understanding.

Making the journey to the temple regularly, he was always surprised at how light the burden of his shell was after his trip. In the temple he couldn't feel his shell on his back nor see himself at all. But as time passed, the weight of his shell would grow heavier, until he felt the urge to return to the temple.

*O*ne day he stood before the pond as he had done so many times before. He cleared his mind and directed himself to let go, then he felt the familiar whoosh of him passing into the misty, esoteric world of transformation. Looking through the clouds, he took the steps steadily making his way through the Halls of Wisdom, passing the Great Hall of Antiquity to the four precious rooms of the universal desires of mankind.

Before him was the room where love was held. He longed to go back to the room, but he was not ready. He remembered vividly the day that he approached this room to have it open as if magic were all around him.

Tag stood before the Room of Compassion waiting expectantly, but nothing happened. He waited a bit longer before moving from side to side, thinking that he could step somehow and it would open. The door did not budge. He waited and he waited, but still nothing happened. The door stood motionless and Tag did not know what to do.

$\mathcal{T}$hen miraculously the door quivered and rippled, distorting and undulating until it was transfigured into a beautiful circle of color and light, moving in waves around him. In the center of the circle was a lock surrounded by four wheels or were they more circles? He did not know. What an odd looking keyhole he thought, but how do I get in? The metamorphosis startled Tag, and he was very upset. He had been so inspired by the Room of Love. He knew that he had to see what was in this room, but could see no way into it. There was no key that let him enter. He paced the halls trying to find the key to the Door of Compassion. There was no key, no magic button or knob to let him in. He grew increasingly frustrated and heavy of heart as he decided to return to the garden.

*J*ust as he turned to go he heard a familiar voice in the center of his being.

**"Tag, to be healed, feel my wound
in the soft spot within the circle
of your compassion."**

Tag paused, "Now, what does that mean?" he questioned. There was no reply. He thought about it again, but he could find no meaning to the message. Puzzled, Tag looked at the beautiful door, which remained closed to him. He felt even more frustrated as he turned to make his way down the long cool hall of compassion. He felt disappointed in his inability to understand the message, because he now understood this to be the key to the room.

Tag returned to the Great Halls of Antiquity and asked what he might do to find the answer to the riddle and the key to the door. He asked the Source of All Things for wisdom in deciphering the message, knowing he could not go on to the next room without having entered this one.

*H*e closed his eyes and his shell and body disappeared, and as always, he was startled at the transition. He waited patiently for a reply. As usual, the great crystal pillars illuminated and the light grew stronger, and energy flowed in and around him. The floor to the room was transparent, and glittered with a thousand veins of energy. His heart quickened in anticipation of the presence of knowledge from the depths of antiquity. Then the voice spoke, or was it a thought entering his very depth of being.

**"Tag, to be healed, feel my wound
in the soft spot within the circle
of your compassion."**

He winced as he heard the now familiar message repeated to him. He waited for more, but nothing more came to him. Turning, saddened by the experience, he left the Great Hall. As he moved away, Tag could feel the presence of the Source of All Things and another message made itself known.

"Be not sad, now is the time for contemplation. Go to the garden, wait, and observe for understanding will come in time."

Tag sighed and left the Hall of Wisdom, making his way down the steps of the temple and through the clouds and mist of time. Then the familiar whoosh and he found himself in the very same spot looking at the deep, pitch-black waters that formed the pond.

He looked up at the water that flowed from the rocks, and the creatures that fluttered around him as he began to move through the garden in a deep funk. He was unable to remove the sadness within him as was suggested by the Source of All Things.

Days passed and Tag was increasingly frustrated by his inability to understand the message that he was now certain was the key to entering the Room of Compassion. He could go no further; he wanted desperately to go on to the next room.

*H*e sat by the lilac bush trying to eat a grub, but it stuck in his throat. To make matters worse that pesky hummingbird kept dive-bombing him repeatedly. Finally he could take no more. "Sam, stop doing that!" he commanded. "Why do you do that anyway? I'm not bothering you." The little hummingbird puffed himself up, neck reddening and boomed, "Stay away from my nourishment!" he demanded darting around the lilac bush. Tag was surprised that such a little creature could be so aggressive.

He shook his head, "I don't care anything about your nourishment," he said growing very angry. "Besides, this garden is full of nourishment and there is plenty enough for everyone." He could feel his anger and voice rise and was immediately contrite. This was not like Tag and he was very embarrassed by his behavior. He took a deep breath and moved away from the tiny creature that dived at him again and again.

Softening his voice a bit, he said, "What's your problem, anyway?"

Sam roared like thunder, "I need this nourishment." Then becoming more restrained, he stated firmly, "I'll die without it!" He was convinced that this was fact.

Tag was astonished, as he sat motionless watching Sam scurry from flower to flower hunting the golden fluid.

He was beginning to understand that he could not meet force with force, and thought a moment before he asserted himself. "Mr. Sam, ahem, excuse me sir, could I offer a suggestion, please."

*B*uzzing frantically, Sam stopped, and sat on a tree limb where he could guard his precious bush and looked down at Tag. "Well, what is it?" Sam said impatiently. "I have a lot to do to keep my nourishment coming in."

$\mathcal{T}$ag was startled by his gruffness, but ventured forward unafraid. "Well, just an observation." He repeated his message. "There is a lot of nourishment in this garden. Lots of different ways to get nourished too! There is so much that there is plenty enough for everyone and I know that the Great Mother will continue to provide for us. So, why don't you just relax and enjoy it? Besides the more you scurry around the more you need. Don't you see that?" Inspired, Tag continued, "I want to be your friend and that is nourishing too!"

Sam listened intently, then abruptly rose up fluttering vigorously and dive-bombed him one more time.

"What do you know; you're not even a hummingbird... Stay away from my nourishment!" he blasted him again.

$\mathcal{B}$ut I can nourish you too," Tag whispered in a small voice as he walked away feeling sad and rejected. He wandered for days thinking about Sam and how he protected his source of sustenance. He wanted to show him that there were other ways to get nourished, and that he was willing to give Sam some of his. He tried as hard as he could to get Sam to stop and pay attention to him, but alas he could not. Sam was caught, spiraling downward in a circle of fear.

Tag was distraught and he talked to the other creatures in the garden about his feelings. Each had a different philosophy about Sam's behavior. "Leave him alone," the wise old owl said sternly, "What do you expect of a hummingbird? This is what they do, and you can't change that now can you?" "No," Tag stammered, "but I'm not trying to change that he is a hummingbird. I just want to talk to him a bit. I think his feathers have interesting features and I want to look more closely," he said sadly. He knew Mr. Owl was not convinced of his motivation and if the truth were known Tag really wasn't sure himself. Frustrated, he wandered down the path towards the pond.

Tag had not been able to return to the temple, because he knew there was no point without the key to the Door of Compassion. The temple was a big source of his own sustenance; he began to feel depleted. Suddenly Tag felt a presence near him. He looked up on the hill and there she stood quietly watching him above the water that fell from the rocks.

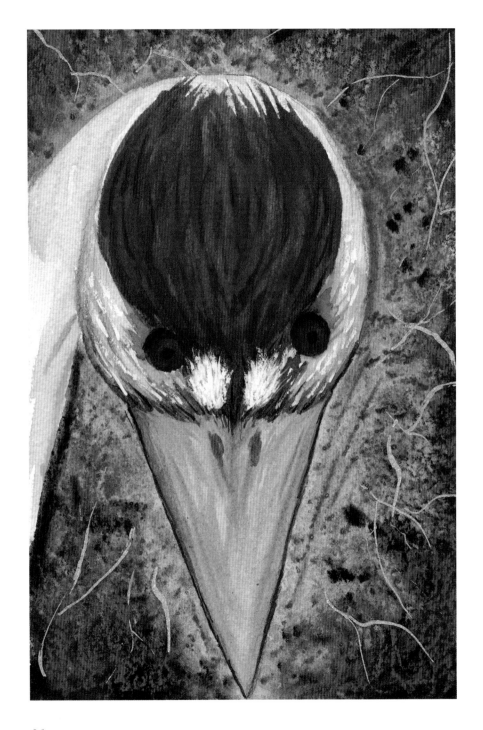

It was his teacher, Ms. Crane; he felt comforted that she was there for him. She seemed to intuitively know everything that went on in the little garden, and most of the time, she was there when he needed her. He paused waiting for her to speak, somehow knowing that she had something important to tell him.

"Tag," she said in her melodic, mystical voice, "feel Sam's need at the center of your being. Make a space in your heart for him to be as he is, then and only then will you both be free."

Tag blinked furiously as he remembered the words from the Source of All Things.

**"Tag, to be healed, feel my wound
in the soft spot within the circle
of your compassion."**

He stood there feeling very still and thought about this for a long time, and then began to wander aimlessly again.

As one day stretched into the next, he watched Sam flit and flutter from one sacred bush and flower to the next. Not once did Sam look at him. He felt very sad indeed. Then one magical day he felt a great weight lift from him and he knew he could return to the temple and the Door of Compassion would be open. He was compassion itself.

As he drifted around the magic garden he saw Ms. Crane standing patiently watching him move up the path.

"So Tag, what have you learned from this experience?"

Tag smiled and moved closer. "Well," he said, "I have learned that you can't change anyone else, and I wouldn't even want to." She made another step towards him, "And?"

He continued, "I can only change myself, and in doing so, I change every thing around me."

"Is that so," she crooned, "can you elaborate?"

Tag breathed deeply and felt very sure of this thought. "My gift to Sam is to understand who he is and then let him be that self. In that way I validate him as a hummingbird. So if he acknowledges me as a turtle, then the work begins of getting my turtle self and his hummingbird self to work in harmony together."

"Interesting, Tag, so what happens if he doesn't acknowledge you as a turtle?"

"Then I can still accept the nature of a hummingbird," Tag said resoundingly sure of himself.

"*G*ood, Tag," Ms. Crane responded, "but there is more to the process of transformation. I think you are now ready for the next room, the Room of Affection."

*T*ag was inspired by Ms. Crane's confidence that he should search for the Room of Affection. He went directly to the pond, following the path to the water's edge. Staring into the water he leaped in without a thought or any preparation. There he stood in the middle of the mist of time looking up at the temple looming grandly before him. Not for one moment did Tag think of what he should do next. Simply reacting, he walked up the steps and down the hall of wisdom to the door of the Room of Affection and entered boldly.

The door opened easily, nothing blocked his path. Entering the room he looked around, stepping into the center with pure abandon. Again he stood waiting for what, he did not know. He felt nothing unusual. Shrugging to himself, he walked around looking at the empty room.

Exploring every square inch, he traced each corner looking for whatever was supposed to be there. He felt no different, no different at all. After a time, he realized with dismay that nothing was going to happen. There was nothing there for him. He made his way to the Great Hall, but did not stop.

An intuition of sorts grabbed at the very depths of his being. He now understood that he was in such a hurry to visit the next room that he did not prepare himself. Tag took no instruction, asked no questions and truly did not know what he was looking for at all. Sick at heart, he followed the path through the halls of wisdom, finding himself back in the midst of time, and feeling a bit sheepish.

At the water's edge, he breathed in a deep sigh. "What happened?" he thought to himself. "I guess I was so eager to go on to the next room that I got caught up in the rush of things." He amused even himself, and stood there chuckling. Shaking his head in wonder, "How did I ever get this far?" He truly did not know. At that moment, he knew what he needed to do and went in search of Ms. Crane.

$\mathcal{M}$s. Crane was waiting for him, a warm smile on her face and a look of amusement in her eyes. "Ah Tag, you have a question in your heart?" Tag looked at her with new respect. She always seemed to know what was going on, so he didn't bother to go through his trip to the temple. He simply asked the obvious, "What do I need to do to find the Room of Affection?" She grinned widely and said, "Well Tag, this room is different than the others." Tag shifted his weight from foot, to foot, to foot, leaning back on the forth a bit as they looked at each other. She never mentioned his impetuousness, and he preferred to ignore it. She simply began to explain what he needed to do.

"Tag, I can't help you with this room. You will need to find the Great Mother to help you locate the Room of Affection." "The Great Mother?" he repeated. "Yes, Tag, the Great Mother, the Mother of the Universe, of Wisdom, of Self-Mastery, and of Time. She takes many forms, and has many faces, although they say no one has ever really lifted her veil. She just takes a form that you can understand. She is the clear light of heaven that breaks the hypnosis instilled by the mesmerizing elements of living. The originator of life will bring forth what you seek. You will find her here, within the garden," she offered.

Tag stood staring at Ms. Crane in disbelief. He was trying hard to take in what she was saying, but could hardly believe his ears, that is, if he had any from which to hear. "I am to go in search of the Mother of the Universe," he repeated dumbfounded. He felt queasy as he stood there waiting to ask the next, and most obvious question." "Where might I find the Mother of the Universe?" he asked tentatively, not sure he wanted to know.

"Ah Tag, that is a good question." she said in a rather animated fashion. "She lives in the cave by the water's edge," she said matter-of-factly. Tag thought a moment, sure he had never seen a cave by the big pond. Anticipating his question she continued. "Look for an ancient stand of trees. In the middle of these trees stands the *oldest* tree, they call her the 'Tree of Life.' She guards the entrance to the cave where the Great Mother lives." "Oh," Tag said, feeling a bit faint of heart. "Go along now Tag, that is all I know, the rest is up to you now" and she was gone.

Tag stood motionless thinking of Ms. Crane's directions, sure he had never seen the trees nor the cave at any time during his travels. He paused, shifting his weight and feeling anticipatory of the coming adventure. He was certain this was the most complicated part of his journey up to now and was getting a bit anxious. "A visit to the Great Mother, the 'nurse' of all time, the Mother of Redemption," the thought shook him to his very depths.

Taking another deep breath, he tried to abate his growing feelings of fear. Wandering around the garden he wondered how he would ever find the trees, the cave and the Great Mother. "I don't remember ever seeing anything like those ancient trees," he muttered to himself.

Then Tag stopped and searched himself. He went deep within, raising his spirit higher and higher. He seemed to be able to survey the entire garden. Everything looked very small. He could see the water that fell from the rocks, the trees, paths; everything was visible through his center. But no where did he see anything like the ancient trees and the cave where the Great Mother resides.

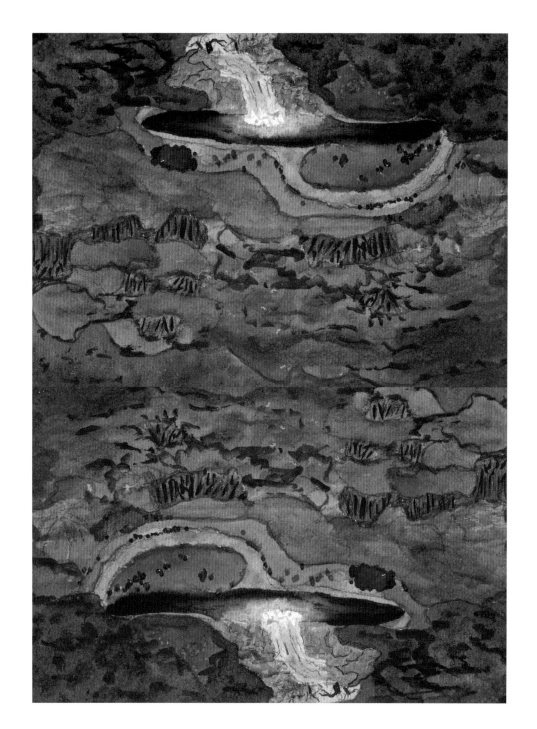

*T*ag felt himself settle back into his center and opened his eyes. He was before the pond, and he decided to walk around the blue bush in his path, not remembering ever seeing that particular flowering kind before. Such beautiful flowers, he thought to himself, absent-mindedly.

Looking up he was completely startled. There she was, straddling the top of a rocky mound, like a great matriarch, her courtesans lining the terrain behind her. All were standing guard to the entrance of a small, rather unobtrusive cave. Tag wondered why someone as special as the Great Mother would be hidden away in such a place. The ancient ones stood ever vigilant guarding the mouth of the cave with dignity and grace. The Sepiroth gleamed brightly like a great beacon, beckoning to him.

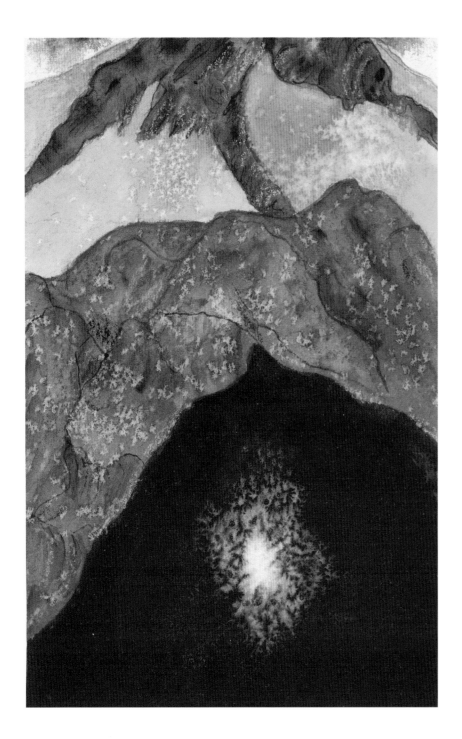

*H*e stood struck by the awesome sight, unsure his legs would carry him any further. But somewhere inside came an urgency to continue. He began the climb up the path to the entrance of the cave. Tag peered through the darkness into the vastness of time and space. There a light began to form in the center of the darkness. Tag did not hesitate at all. He stepped through the portal and into the center of time itself.

He felt the cold dampness of the cave engulf him, and he shuddered remembering his first experience with a cave in the garden of the great creatures. He remembered the beast that lived in the cave and he could feel the weight of his anxiety fill him up. His legs were like lead as he moved through the damp tunnels towards the light.

There in the immense cavern, the light grew very bright and flashed a bold and powerful display. A great wind blew up and stirred the center of the cavern. The beautiful and awesome light shimmered. At its fulcrum, a magnificent woman stood stately and austere, as she spoke to him.

"What would you ask of me?" she said simply. Her voice was terrifying, yet gentle and gracious. Tag wanted to run, but stood his ground without flinching. There was no way he would shrink from the demands of this trial he thought to himself. He would stand tall and ask for what he wanted.

"Mother of the Universe, clear light of heaven, illuminator of the great trials, unifier of intelligence, I do have a question," he stated evenly. "Where might I find the Room of Affection?"

A hush came over everything in the cavern, and the quiet was deafening. Radiating a beautiful, powerful energy that illuminated the great cave, she warmed everything around him. He felt a sense of peace sweep over him like he never felt before.

*T*hen he was suddenly struck by the answer. Of course, it isn't a place at all, but a gift of acceptance that you give to everyone with words and deeds.

Affection is a state of mind that comes of truly seeing every creature with new eyes. When you see into their souls, you are compelled to give affection because you are seeing the purest part of who they are, not what they have been or are to become. This state of being is completely innocent, given freely and unconditionally. Much like the babies of the garden, who give without thinking, through touch, smile, and unabashed warmth.

Tag stood in the power and majesty of her presence, the glow of her reaching into the depths of him. How can he be feeling these things? It was the strangest experience, yet, he was terrified and full of peace at the same time, he mused to himself. Then as suddenly as she appeared, the light faded into a pitch-black darkness that consumed him. Tag quickly hurried back the way he came, running into the walls of the cave as he made his way towards the light of the entrance and into the peaceful little garden.

$\mathcal{H}$e looked around him, wondering if anyone noticed his scurrying through the cave and his obvious anxiety. No one seemed to pay him any attention at all. Life just went on as usual, everyone doing what they always did, playing, gathering their food, and living their lives. Tag stood feeling the intensity of the moment. He felt at peace as he watched life happen before his eyes.

*T*ime passed and the entrance to the next room had not become visible to Tag. He grew impatient as he searched everywhere for a door, portal or anything leading him in the right direction. For the first time since he found the enchanted garden, he walked up the path and outside the circle of safety. He was still surrounded by the light, and had not yet reached the wailing winter that he left above him some months before.

He looked down the path that led out of the magic garden. Although he had not completed the process of transformation, he felt compelled to challenge his boundaries. Standing there he pressed against the walls of time, searching for what was to be his final trial.

Exploring the Room of Impartiality seemed incomprehensible. "What did 'impartiality' mean anyway?" He was beginning to panic as he realized that each room became increasingly more difficult to penetrate. If logic followed, this would be the hardest trial to master. He stood in the middle of the path, painfully aware of the challenge that lay ahead. Then turning around, he made his way back to the safety of the garden and the challenge that awaited him.

Tag walked the paths of the garden searching daily for a clue to the next room. He looked for Ms. Crane, but he knew this time he was utterly on his own. Whatever he needed was within him, all he needed to do was to access the part of him that knows.

He sat still by the water's edge and tried to clear his thoughts, to let go of control for a few moments. He desperately wanted Ms. Crane's guidance, but he instinctively knew that part of the trial was to let inner direction be his guide. He stood still and willed himself to *just be.*

In that moment he knew what he was to do next. He would return to the cave, and the Great Mother of Redemption. He felt dizzy as he contemplated a return.

One would think that having had the experience once, it would make it easier to do again, but that was not the case. The sweet mystery of the force of her will as the illuminator of the trials made her so illustrious that it struck fear in his heart. He felt ashamed of the fear, for she deserved only his love and respect.

As he contemplated returning to the cave, he realized he had a problem. Where was that blue bush anyway? This was the signpost that led to the Tree of Life and the entrance to the cave. He wandered, obsessed by the desire to find the blue bush. The exquisite trumpet shaped sky blue and purple colored flowers were like no other that he had seen thus far.

He moved up and down trails looking high and low for the blossoming bush. Trying to recreate the last moments before his discovery, he remembered raising his spirits higher and higher, while he surveyed the terrain of the garden.

In a flash of memory he recreated his steps. The blue bush appeared before his mind's eye like magic. Smiling to himself, he felt powerful, very powerful indeed!

Renewed and energized, he pushed forward, rounding the bush, and there they were! The majestic 'Tree of Life' and her courtesans, the ancient ones took Tag's breath away.

Once again he felt small and insignificant. Antiquity stood before his eyes and the sight dazzled him. Humbly, he made his way towards the opening of the cave, knowing that he would have an experience like no other.

There he paused at the entrance as he watched the light form as it did before, into a powerful burst of energy. Although he was quaking with every step, he moved steadily towards the light. He was obsessed by the desire to complete the trials.

The dampness of the cave chilled him to the bone and he felt stiff as he moved through the cold corridors towards the cavern. The closer he got, the slower he moved, and he became increasingly fearful of the coming experience that he knew in his heart of hearts would forever change him.

The last part of the Ceremony had begun and there was no turning back, not that he wanted to, he had definitely come too far. The change was inevitable and welcomed.

*T*ag moved toward the light and the entrance to the great room, the cavern where the Mother of Redemption resided. The light was soft and smaller than before, just a whisper, centered in the cavern about four or five feet above the floor of the room. It illuminated only the space around him and no more. As the light grew, he could see the outline of a young woman, her flowing hair, and the light radiating out of her hand like a magic wand. Surprise overshadowed the intensity of the fear and he stood watching her beautiful form illuminate the cavern. He remembered Ms. Crane's words, "No one has ever really lifted her veil, she simply takes a form that you can understand."

Tag watched the beautiful, ageless young woman breathe new life into him. He was filled with a peace and love that he could not explain. Enjoying the moment, he did nothing but stare foolishly at her presence. She generated such energy and power that it filled him with sublime wonder. There in the darkness of the cave and the beauty of the moment, he completely trusted that he would make it through the next trial.

The wisdom of the Universe settled into his spirit, allowing him to experience the next part of the trial in comfort. He asked the younger version of the Great Mother to work her magic. "Mother of the mysteries of life, unifier of intelligence, what gifts do you have for me today?"

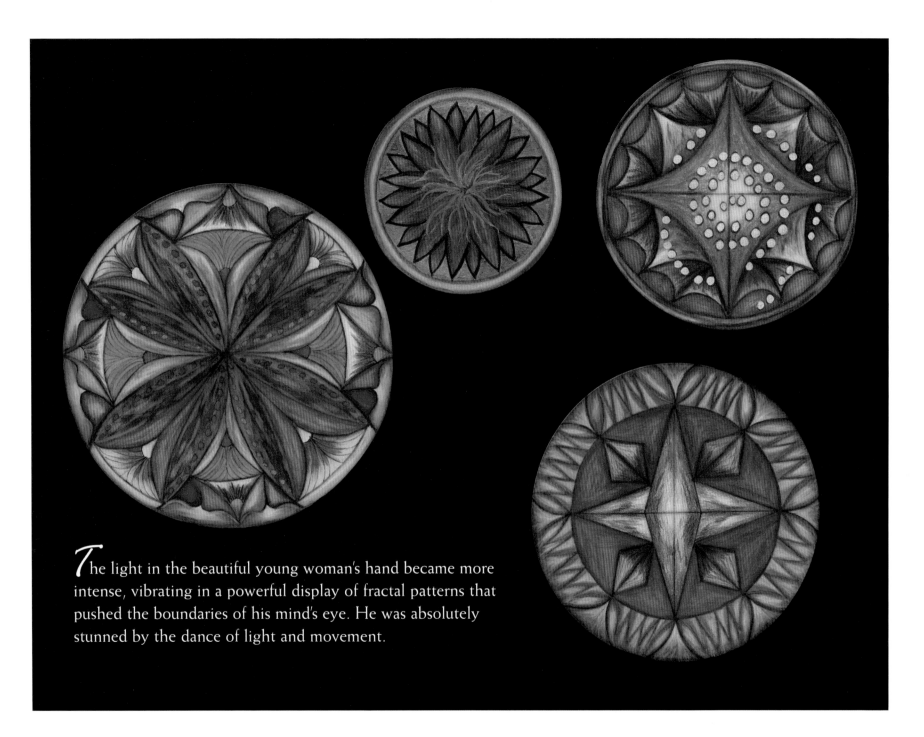

*T*he light in the beautiful young woman's hand became more intense, vibrating in a powerful display of fractal patterns that pushed the boundaries of his mind's eye. He was absolutely stunned by the dance of light and movement.

There in the center from time to time he could see flashes of the beautiful young woman, hair blowing in the winds of time, fire radiating around her in a passionate display of her all-consuming beauty.

Tag stood in an esoteric moment of wonder waiting for what, he did not know. He asked again, this time in an emotion-filled whisper: "What gifts do you have for me today?" Then a response of knowledge came swiftly.

The task before you is to RE-member from where you come. To pull together all of the lost parts of Self without losing the beauty of antiquity's presence. In the stillness of this moment, the knowledge of the Universe is yours. Be of good cheer dear one. We love you as *no* other and as *all* others. We are one in this.

Tag stood firm in the presence of divine knowledge, letting the message seep into his heart. He knew in a flash the meaning of the message and wanted to cement the knowledge into a corner of his heart. He would never want to lose the thoughts and feelings generated by this revelation.

The beauty and majesty of the time humbled him and he bowed before the magnificence of all he was experiencing. Tag held the knowledge of the Universe within his heart for all of the creatures of the enchanted garden and the creatures that live above where the winter wailed in fury.

He watched as the light moved gently back to a soft stream surrounding the beautiful young woman who then faded into the darkness.

Although he could see nothing, he was not the least bit afraid. Turning around, he traced his footsteps back along the corridors of the cave and out into the beautiful little garden. He was energized and peaceful as he walked into day light. Moving down the path to the water's edge, Tag thought about what had happened in the cave.

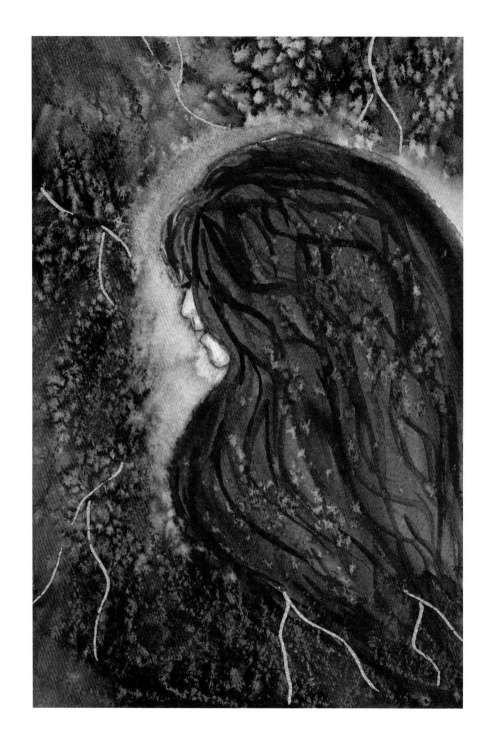

*T*ag wandered through the garden in a peaceful haze letting the messages from all of the rooms settle gently into his heart. He visited from time to time with his friends as they went about their daily lives, oblivious of the trials; the rooms that were now a part of him or the sense of wonder for which he had been blessed. He traced the experience that he had along the corners of his mind. The rooms offered an opportunity to see the world and everything in it in a new way. Standing at the water's edge, he looked at the water that fell from the rocks and the creatures that inhabited the peaceful and enchanted little garden as he had done countless times before.

*T*hen he knew it was time to move on with his life. The trials were over, at least these trials, and his life was just beginning. "Now he would use what he knew to bless himself and all that he met," he thought walking up the path towards the top of the ridge.

He stopped part way and looked in wonder at the beautiful garden. The spray of the falls dampened the path that led out of the protected space.

At the top he looked back at the tracks that he left in the steps leading to where he would exit the little garden. He had tried to miss the tiniest of the flowers in the path, noticing with mild irritation that as it happens in life, he had unavoidably crushed a few along the way.

Smiling to himself, he surveyed the tracks, the creatures of the garden and the beauty all around him. He did not say goodbye, not even to Ms. Crane. They were all a part of him now, leaving footprints at the center of his soul as he left his prints in the path below.

As Tag stood viewing the full spectrum of the garden, he thought about what he had learned while exploring all of the Rooms of Man's Great Desires. Each room showed him how he might live a more peaceful and enriched life.

Within the Room of Love he was shown that at some level we are all equal and one with the Universe. Each of us possesses the ability to unite to form the essence of *pure* love. Every room helped him to discern some important part of himself. With compassion we make a gift to others of understanding that lets them be who they are at a given moment in time. Tag grimaced as he remembered the events in the garden after his experience with Sam. He thought the lesson was for Sam, but it was for Tag. When he validated Sam, he also validated himself.

The other two rooms were equally important centering points for his life. The Room of Affection he thought to himself, is a gift of acceptance that we give to everyone we meet with words and deeds. In this state of mind we truly see every one in a new way, and give to them freely and unconditionally. Then in the last room, the task before him in the Room of Impartiality was to RE-member from where he comes; to pull together all of the lost parts of Self without losing the beauty of antiquity's presence. To understand how we are connected to the earth and to the Universe.

*T*ag walked out of the garden and into the clear light of day. Spring had come to the valley and everything was in full bloom. He breathed in the fresh scent of the new, rich world that awaited him, trusting life to be sweetly filled with whatever was the flip side of things, as promised in the Room of Love. He adjusted himself to the coming story that would be his life. Making his way down the path towards the unknown, he could now let the full beauty of the Universe shine through his soul.

The End

Epilogue

There in a moment of grace, Tag pressed against the boundaries of his soul to see a compelling reflection of Self, and because he was able to accept what he saw with affection and compassion, he was healed. We are on this Earth School to unlearn those things that keep us from remembering who we are and why we came here, to experience our humanity and complete whatever unique work we have volunteered to do.

This is the dance of light we do together and the energy that is exchanged between two people in any relationship, friend or foe assists in this integration. Whenever a relationship is between gender opposites, the process sways between masculine and feminine, the yin and the yang, the anima and animus. The more powerful the energy of attraction, the more it wants to complete itself in integration. So it is that the soul looks at its reflection, its imago or mirror image, seeing all that is held latent in its shadow.

The stronger the emotions, either positive or negative, the more they reflect a part of the self that wants to be recognized and remembered. In giving that recognition, allowing the feelings to bubble to the surface, whatever they might be, some part of the work of the soul is accomplished.

Thus the process empowers us, freeing, energizing, and revealing the authentic Self we were born with. This creates a capacity to give freely and completely, and connect in ways that nourish. In the midst of the dance we invoke a beauty so powerful that it lights up the Universe in harmony, cooperation and a respect for all living things.

Notes

Notes

Notes

Notes